ideals AMERICANA

This great broad land of ours: its sweeping plains,
Its rivers deep and long, its mountain chains,
Enchant my enraptured heart with joy and pride
And set me roving free from tide to tide.

I love its snow-clad peaks, its lakes of blue,
Its golden dawnings, and its morning dew.
I cherish every road that leads me far
Toward crimson sunset and bright evening star.

I've known its summer heat, its winter cold,
As through its length and breadth I've gaily strolled.
I've seen it stretched below as from the air;
I've watched it, like a map, unroll down there.

Its flowering desert sands, its mighty trees,
I've taken to my heart as one who sees
Them as his gifts from God, whose lavish hand
Has decked with living gems this lovely land.

Oh, would that all who live within its bound
Could realize that they're on holy ground,
And that our lives would then as comely be
As is America ... land of the free.

Lewis Parker Miller

ISBN 0-8249-1004-4 350

IDEALS—Vol. 38, No. 5 July MCMLXXXI. IDEALS (ISSN 0019-137X) is published eight times a year,
January, February, April, June, July, September, October, November
by IDEALS PUBLISHING CORPORATION, 11315 Watertown Plank Road, Milwaukee, Wis. 53226
Second class postage paid at Milwaukee, Wisconsin. Copyright © MCMLXXXI by IDEALS PUBLISHING CORPORATION.
Postmaster, please send form 3579 to Ideals Publishing Corporation, Post Office Box 2100, Milwaukee, Wis. 53201
All rights reserved. Title IDEALS registered U.S. Patent Office.
Published simultaneously in Canada.

ONE-YEAR SUBSCRIPTION—eight consecutive issues as published—$15.95
TWO-YEAR SUBSCRIPTION—sixteen consecutive issues as published—$27.95
SINGLE ISSUES—$3.50

Publisher, James A. Kuse

Managing Editor, Ralph Luedtke

Editor/Ideals, Colleen Callahan Gonring

Associate Editor, Linda Robinson

Production Manager, Mark Brunner

Photographic Editor, Gerald Koser

Copy Editor, Barbara Nevid

Art Editor, Duane Weaver

Invocation of the Dawn

Look to this day!
For it is life, the very life of life.
In its brief course lie all the verities,
All the realities of existence:
The bliss of growth,
The glory of action,
The splendor of beauty;

For yesterday is always a dream,
And tomorrow is only a vision;
But today, well-lived,
Makes every yesterday a dream of happiness
And every tomorrow a dream of hope.
Look well, therefore, to this day.

Kalidasa

VOICE
OF
AMERICA

Stella Craft Tremble

I am the cornfields of the Middle West,
Rustling and whispering in the prairie breeze,
The snow-capped Rockies pointing to the sky.
I am youth's ambitions, symbols of these:

The cotton fields and bluegrass of the South
That stand for gracious hospitality,
The spirit of undefeated statehood
And antebellum aristocracy.

I am the rolling voice of crested waves
Inviting all within my Golden Gate,
The vast Pacific of the vibrant West,
With shore and climate sure to captivate.

Continued

I am America! Its eastern towns,
Its rocky hillsides and its winding streams,
The sacrifices of Founding Fathers
With torch to light the pathway to their dreams.

I am the cities: New York, Chicago,
All magic towns of our wondrous nation.
I am the flag that proudly waves aloft
For freedom and its commemoration.

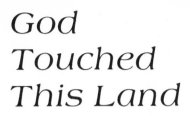

God Touched This Land

A Salute to the Hostages

America, we see you stand
A vibrant, awe-inspiring land.
Your zeal inspires; your dreams uplift,
But freedom is your greatest gift.

On, on they came from land and shore
To see the lamp, the open door.
With words eternal, man decreed
That Freedom's rights are guaranteed.

God-fearing men with virtuous wives
Soon read the weather in the skies,
Strung their fences, plowed their lands,
Held the future in their hands.

Time moves along, a transient dream,
As leafy vessels ford a stream.
Other interests cast their spell
Till Freedom sounds a warning bell.

Our countrymen were boldly seized
To bring this nation to its knees.
As hearts were touched, they chose to share,
And knees were bent in common prayer.

United—We, the People—learned
When fifty-two at last returned
That Freedom shared will stand the strain.
We SHALL NOT be misused again!

God touched this land—a spirit, free—
With yellow ribbons on each tree,
Smiles and tears, a sounding bell.
Who honors Freedom, guards it well!

1981 © Alice Leedy Mason

Beauty

He has given beauty in all that grows:
In the bright-hued begonia, the perfumed rose,
In the lacy vines a keen eye discerns,
In the pale green avenue of tall ferns.
Beauty, beauty's in all we see:
Beauty blooming on every tree,
Beauty of day, beauty of night,
Beauty of stars, the silk moonlight,
A rugged beauty in mountains of stone,
An awesome beauty in deserts alone,

Sunsets which take your breath away,
Shimmering dawns, golden or gray,
Sparkling blue lakes like rapture's dreams,
Rushing rivers or singing streams,
Or snow falling gently on upturned face,
Pattering rain like a loving embrace.
There's nothing in beauty tempting ire;
Everything's there to meet our desire,
For beauty is an alluring star.

Hazelle R. Paus

Walt Whitman

Walt Whitman, born in 1819, was a literary pioneer, exploring, celebrating, and elevating life. Whitman's poetry was a departure from the structured poetic form of his day, and his early works met with some criticism. In search of the solitude afforded by nature, Whitman rambled throughout the hills and woodlands of America. He wrote about nature and was particularly fond of prescribing its silence and simplicity for all human endeavors. The poet explored a country founded on freedom for each person, and he continually sang the praises of the common man and woman. He was fascinated with people much like his own father, a Brooklyn carpenter, and his mother, who in her youth could mount a horse and till the fields. Hardworking, uneducated, and free Americans are the heroes of Whitman's poetry. He had seen firsthand the result of democracy gone awry. During the Civil War, he traveled to the battlefront to search for his brother and stayed on as a volunteer nurse, administering to the wounded and dying. In many ways, this war became the focal point of Whitman's work. The poetry of Walt Whitman reminds us that each person is unique—a combination of all he has seen, heard and done. In reading Whitman's poems, we join the poet in his quest, in his celebration of life, of man, and of democracy.

Afoot and lighthearted I take to the open road,
Healthy, free, the world before me,
The long brown path before me leading wherever I choose.

Henceforth I ask not good fortune, I myself am good fortune,
Henceforth I whimper no more, postpone no more, need nothing,
Done with indoor complaints, libraries, querulous criticisms,
Strong and content I travel the open road.

The earth, that is sufficient,
I do not want the constellations any nearer,
I know they are very well where they are,
I know they suffice for those who belong to them.

The earth expanding right hand and left hand,
The picture alive, every part in its best light,
The music falling in where it is wanted,
    and stopping where it is not wanted,
The cheerful voice of the public road,
    the gay fresh sentiment of the road.

O highway I travel, do you say to me, "Do not leave me"?
Do you say, "Venture not—if you leave me you are lost"?
Do you say, "I am already prepared,
    I am well-beaten and undenied, adhere to me"?

O public road, I say back
    I am not afraid to leave you, yet I love you,
You express me better than I can express myself,
You shall be more to me than my poem.

I think heroic deeds were all conceived in the open air,
    and all free poems also,
I think I could stop here myself and do miracles,
I think whatever I shall meet on the road I shall like,
    and whoever beholds me shall like me,
I think whoever I see must be happy.

There was a child
went forth every day,
And the first object
that he look'd upon,
that object he became,
And that object
became part of him
for the day
or a certain part of the day,
Or for many years
or stretching cycles of years.

In all people I see myself, none more
and not one a barley-corn less,
And the good or bad I say of myself
I say of them. . . .
I am the poet of the Body
And I am the poet of the Soul,
The pleasures of heaven are with me
And the pains of hell are with me,
The first I graft and increase upon myself,
The latter I translate into a new tongue.

Give me the splendid silent sun
　　with all his beams full-dazzling,
Give me juicy autumnal fruit ripe
　　and red from the orchard,
Give me a field where the unmowed grass grows,
Give me an arbor, give me the trellised grape,
Give me fresh corn and wheat,
　　give me serene-moving animals teaching content,
Give me nights perfectly quiet
　　as on high plateaus west of the Mississippi,
　　and I looking up at the stars,
Give me odorous at sunrise a garden
　　of beautiful flowers where I can walk undisturbed,
Give me for marriage a sweet-breathed woman
　　of whom I should never tire,
Give me a perfect child, give me a way aside
　　from the noise of the world, a rural domestic life,
Give me to warble spontaneous songs
　　recluse by myself, for my own ears only,
Give me solitude, give me Nature,
　　give me again, O Nature, your primal sanities!

A child said *What is the grass?*
fetching it to me with full hands,
How could I answer the child?
I do not know what it is
any more than he.

I guess it must be the flag of my disposition,
out of hopeful green stuff woven.

Or I guess it is the handkerchief of the Lord,
A scented gift and remembrancer designedly dropt,
Bearing the owner's name someway in the corners,
that we may see and remark, and say *Whose?*
Or I guess the grass is itself a child,
the produced babe of the vegetation.

Do you see, O my brothers and sisters?
It is not chaos or death—it is form, union, plan—
it is eternal life—
it is happiness.

Here is the test of wisdom,
Wisdom is not finally tested in schools,
Wisdom cannot be pass'd from one having it to another not having it,
Wisdom is of the soul, is not susceptible of proof, is its own proof,
Applies to all stages and objects and qualities and is content,
Is the certainty of the reality and immortality of things,
　　and the excellence of things;
Something there is in the float of the sight of things
　　that provokes it out of the soul.

A noiseless, patient spider,
I mark'd where, on a little promontory, it stood isolated,
Mark'd how, to explore the vacant vast surrounding,
It launched forth filament, filament, filament, out of itself,
Ever unreeling them—ever tirelessly speeding them.

And you O my Soul where you stand,
Surrounded, detached, in measureless oceans of space,
Ceaselessly musing, venturing, throwing, seeking the spheres to connect them,
Till the bridge you will need be form'd, till the ductile anchor hold,
Till the gossamer thread you fling catch somewhere, O my Soul.

Amid the valleys of the Golden West,
    Where gleam the thriving cities of the bay,
Where distant mountains lift their rugged crest
    To guard the fertile site of San Jose,
Here have the founders traversed the domain
    To plant their shrines on wooded hill and slope,
Here have the padres trudged the dusty plain
    To ring at last their mission bells of hope.

Here have the wastelands bloomed where they have trod,
    Here stately churches grace the valley sod,
With spires that lift their solemn majesty
    To flame their altars for posterity.

To you the builders, hail and fervent praise
    For shrines erected in these latter days,
For you have pledged His glory to proclaim
    Who dedicate cathedrals to His name.
You ask no banners to inscribe your name,
    Your hall of fame seeks neither bronze or stone,
For you have built where tarnish cannot stain,
    Nor tablets crumble into the unknown.

Dedicatory Ode

Bertha A. Kleinman

May peace brood over this blest abode,
    And this dedication, an episode,
Be etched in the rituals you raise
    As your organed chancels resound with praise.
Your challenge rings to those who follow on,
    To build anew down through the centuries,
To grapple and surmount through all defeat
    And give the world such monuments as these,
That state and nation from such growth and good
    Shall yet be bridged with brotherhood.

Paul Revere's Ride

Henry Wadsworth Longfellow

Listen, my children, and you shall hear
Of the midnight ride of Paul Revere,
On the eighteenth of April, in Seventy-five;
Hardly a man is now alive
Who remembers that famous day and year.

He said to his friend, "If the British march
By land or sea from the town tonight,
Hang a lantern aloft in the belfry arch
Of the North Church tower as a signal light—
One, if by land, and two, if by sea;
And I on the opposite shore will be,
Ready to ride and spread the alarm
Through every Middlesex village and farm,
For the country folk to be up and to arm."

Then he said, "Good night!" and with muffled oar
Silently rowed to the Charlestown shore,
Just as the moon rose over the bay,
Where swinging wide at her moorings lay

The *Somerset*, British man-of-war;
A phantom ship, with each mast and spar
Across the moon like a prison bar,
And a huge black hulk, that was magnified
By its own reflection in the tide.
. . .
Then he climbed to the tower of the Old North Church,
By the wooden stairs, with stealthy tread,
To the belfry-chamber overhead,
And startled the pigeons from their perch
On the somber rafters, that round him made
Masses and moving shapes of shade—
By the trembling ladder, steep and tall,
To the highest window in the wall,
Where he paused to listen and look down
A moment on the roofs of the town,
And the moonlight flowing over all.
. . .
Meanwhile, impatient to mount and ride,
Booted and spurred, with a heavy stride
On the opposite shore walked Paul Revere.
Now he patted his horse's side,
Now gazed at the landscape far and near,
Then, impetuous, stamped the earth,
And turned and tightened his saddle girth;

But mostly he watched with eager search
The belfry tower of the Old North Church,
As it rose above the graves on the hill,
Lonely and spectral and somber and still.
And lo! as he looks on the belfry's height
A glimmer, and then a gleam of light!
He springs to the saddle, the bridle he turns,
But lingers and gazes, till full on his sight
A second lamp in the belfry burns!

A hurry of hoofs in a village street,
A shape in the moonlight, a bulk in the dark,
And beneath, from the pebbles, in passing, a spark
Struck out by a steed flying fearless and fleet:
That was all! And yet, through the gloom and the light,
The fate of a nation was riding that night;
And the spark struck out by that steed, in his flight,
Kindled the land into flame with its heat.
. . .
It was twelve by the village clock,
When he crossed the bridge into Medford town.
He heard the crowing of the cock,
And barking of the farmer's dog,
And felt the damp of the river fog,
That rises after the sun goes down.
. . .
It was two by the village clock,
When he came to the bridge in Concord town.
He heard the bleating of the flock,
And the twitter of birds among the trees,
And felt the breath of the morning breeze
Blowing over the meadows brown.
And one was safe and asleep in his bed
Who at the bridge would be first to fall,
Who that day would be lying dead,
Pierced by a British musket-ball.

You know the rest. In the books you have read
How the British Regulars fired and fled—
How the farmers gave them ball for ball,
From behind each fence and farmyard wall,
Chasing the red-coats down the lane,
Then crossing the fields to emerge again
Under the trees at the turn of the road,
And only pausing to fire and load.

So through the night rode Paul Revere;
And so through the night went his cry of alarm
To every Middlesex village and farm—
A cry of defiance and not of fear,
A voice in the darkness, a knock at the door,
And a word that shall echo for evermore!
For, borne on the night-wind of the Past,
Through all our history, to the last,
In the hour of darkness and peril and need,
The people will awaken and listen to hear
The hurrying hoofbeats of that steed,
And the midnight message of Paul Revere.

The American Flag

Helen Shick

The Stars and Stripes is flying,
And it's waving high and free;
And rightly so, it's the symbol of
Man's love for liberty.

It has earned the name "Old Glory,"
It bears meaning in each star;
There's history in each stripe of red
And in each snow-white bar.

Each star is representing
A state within our nation;
Thirteen at first, now fifty glow
In our mighty constellation.

Our flag is an honored symbol
Of all that has gone before;
It is the ensign of our principles;
It is the guardian of our shores.

It speaks of loyalty and justice
In its field of truest blue;
The snowy white means purity,
And it glows for freedom, too.

The blazing red means courage
And a strength of great renown;
Three colors tell of much sacrifice,
Great deeds and lives laid down.

Old Glory tells the story
Of wise men of another day,
Who used each ounce of wit and brawn
To create our USA.

In our flag we see brave soldiers,
Valiant statesmen are in each seam;
There are families woven in the threads
Who made real the American dream.

We read the Mayflower Compact,
Where democracy cast a sprout;
We hear independence first declared
And the Liberty Bell ring out.

We see the grit of Molly Pitcher,
And Valley Forge's blood and tears,
Bunker Hill and the men who rallied,
And the Civil War's dark fears.

In the Stars and Stripes we honor
We see the pioneers move west;
In the curl of every ripple
We watch Americans put to test.

While the flag is flying proudly,
We see Perry on Erie's shore . . .
Battaan . . . the daring moon walk . . .
The Unknown Soldier and so much more.

We hear wind sweep over plain lands
And glimpse miles of golden wheat;
We know abundance in our granaries;
We hear the heart of labor beat.

We see a land of wealth and plenty . . .
The glow of learning's noble lights . . .
The wheels of industry ever turning . . .
The awesome power of voting rights.

When the Stars and Stripes is waving
This nation's history comes in view;
There is more yet to be written;
Let's keep it good and honorable, too.

The Plot to Kidnap the General

The air was electric with treason. Huddled in the dimly-lit back room of a Bowery Lane tavern, from which they could see the campfires and hear the clatter of General Washington's encampment, the conspirators analyzed every detail of their bold plan. Painstakingly, they probed for the slightest flaw that could thwart it.

There wasn't any. The plot was absolutely foolproof. And as the cabal's candle flickered in the light summer breeze, that evening of June 24, 1776, so did the American Revolution.

If the plan succeeded—and the conspirators had no doubt it would—it would snuff out the rebellion before it ever had a chance to burn brightly and enflame the Colonies. The rebels would be crushed ruthlessly and the rightful authority of His Majesty, George III, would be fully restored.

The conspirators were no crackpots. They represented the very flower of Colonial New York society.

Their leader was no less than William Tryon, Tory governor of New York. His chief aide was David Matthews, New York City's Tory mayor. And behind them were some of the city's outstanding public figures, lawyers, physicians and merchants.

Central figure in the whole plot, however, was Thomas Hickey, one of General Washington's bodyguards. Branded pickpocket and thief before joining the Continental Army, Hickey was the Judas of the lot. While the conspirators were all acting out of conviction and intense loyalty to the Crown, Hickey would be paid 20 guineas for his villainy.

It would be his responsibility, on one pretext or another, to lure the trusting general to a waterfront warehouse. There, a boat would be waiting to spirit Washington to a British warship anchored in the bay.

Once aboard, Washington would be clapped in irons. The vessel would then set sail for British-occupied Boston, where the American commander would be speedily tried, found guilty of high treason and hung on the Boston Common.

It would be a dramatic example for other rebel leaders of what they could expect if they refused to lay down their arms and disband their forces. More than that, Washington was the heart and soul of the American rebellion. With him gone, the Continental Army—a rag-tag, bob tail assortment of citizen soldiers—would be totally leaderless. It would fade away and the American Revolution would die aborning.

There was one final order for Hickey—and another 10 guineas in it for him. If the general resisted his kidnappers, he was to be killed. It would not be nearly as effective a lesson to other rebels as a public trial and hanging. But one way or another, Washington had to be removed.

Their plans set, and fearful of discovery if they delayed too long, the conspirators decided to act immediately. Washington was to be kidnapped the next night. And within a month, the American Revolution would be history.

Solemnly aware of what they were doing and its implications, the conspirators shook hands and left, one by one, by a side door. Last to leave were Hickey and Tryon.

Suddenly, Hickey demanded his "fee" in advance. Tryon flatly refused, knowing full well who and what Hickey was. Give him his fee and he might very well back out of the plot and go his own way.

The two men bickered for more than an hour. Finally, a disgusted Tryon, seeing no other way out, gave in and promised to deliver half of Hickey's fee the next morning. He'd receive the other half after he'd completed his assignment.

Hickey, however, never appeared to receive his blood money. By a stroke of fate—one of those twists that always seems to alter history—two of Washington's officers were carousing in a tavern just down the street from the conspirators' meeting place. They decided to head back to camp just when Hickey and Tryon were leaving together.

Tryon's Tory sentiments were well known. And the fact that Washington's bodyguard was in his company immediately triggered the officers' suspicions.

Within an hour, Hickey was under arrest. Grilled by a furious Washington himself,

Hickey confessed all—of course, immediately implicating his co-conspirators in a desperate attempt to save his own neck.

Tyron and the rest of his band, however, were alerted to Hickey's treachery by a spy they had in the Colonial camp. They slipped out of New York on the same ship that was to have carried Washington to his execution.

Next day, a court-martial was convened. It took the assembled officers only five minutes to find the now blubbering bodyguard guilty of treason and to order him hung.

Hickey threw himself on the mercy of the court and begged General Washington for clemency. It's the measure of Washington as a magnificent human being that he wavered and almost commuted Hickey's penalty. Only the determined plea of his aides, who believed that Hickey must serve as an example to other Colonial militiamen turned traitors, stayed his hand.

On the blustery, rain-swept morning of June 28, before a throng of 20,000, Hickey was drummed to the gallows and hung.

General Washington's Orderly Book for the day reported the event. "The fate of Thomas Hickey, executed this day for Mutiny and Treachery, the general intends will be a warning to every soldier in the army to avoid these crimes so disgraceful to the character of a soldier and pernicious to his countrymen, whose pay he receives and bread he eats."

The warning served its purpose. Not another attempt was made on the general's life.

Washington, of course, went on to lead his ragged Colonials to victory and to serve as the nation's first president. His name towers above all others in the annals of the country.

But who, today, recalls Thomas Hickey? Except for a lucky twist of fate, his name might be almost as well remembered as is Washington's, for his role in a plot that certainly would have altered the course of American history.

Harvey J. Berman

Call of the Sea

Joy Belle Burgess

Where the waves rolled in from the sea,
I wandered at peace and alone
Through the veil of thick, gray mist,
The breeze and the white breakers' foam;

With aught but the gulls above me
And the vast ocean-world beyond,
I heard, as the wind came singing,
The call of the sea—the faraway song!

Out where the billows were swelling,
Came the mighty thunder and roar,
The soul-stirring sound of the surf
As it swept across the shore;

Midst the spray of the lone sea-breakers,
The beauty too wondrous to tell,
I waded where wavelets were swirling
And bearing me gifts of pearly white shells.

Where the billowy foam kissed the sand,
I stepped lightly, happy and free,
Lost in the dream and the wonder
Of a paradise isle far over the sea;

While the waves rolled in with their thunder,
The gulls dipped gently and soared,
Still I heard, as the wind came singing,
The beckoning call from a faraway shore!

Village by the Sea
Ruth Linnea Erickson

I like a little seacoast town,
Where in and out, and up and down,
The winding roads run eagerly
Until they reach the open sea;
Then leisurely meander where
The salty tang perfumes the air,
And weathered tars, their voyage done,
Are drying fishnets in the sun.

I like a little harbor best
Where colored sails are furled to rest
And anchored vessels gently rock,
As seamen loll upon the dock;
Where little homes at close of day
See sunset flame across the bay,
And common folk, like you and me,
Hear lullabies from out the sea.

New England Town
Ruth Linnea Erickson

Sleepy, smiling country town,
Drowsing beneath your trees,
Fondly clasping to your heart
The gently lapping seas,
Whose salty brine
Is a mellowed wine
Wafting on the breeze.

Hovering above with arms outflung
Your mighty elm trees rear,
Spreading their branches in embrace
And murmuring in your ear;
Through shaded aisle
Your doorways smile
And sing of yesteryear.

Quaint you are, New England town,
Drowsing beneath your trees;
A little lady dressed in lace
The passing traveler sees,
With gray head bent
In sweet content
With all her memories.

Sunday Chicken Dinner
... An American Tradition

Gladys Taber

Chicken dinner for Sunday has been a tradition in most of our country until recently. In the small town in the Midwest where I grew up, I spent part of the church service thinking of food. The pews were hard and uncomfortable and the sermons were long, the prayers as long as most sermons of today. By the time we finally reached home, I was in a state of starvation. Then came the chicken, fricasseed, with creamy light dumplings and a bowl of golden gravy with giblets sparking it. And also fluffy mashed potatoes and whatever vegetables were in season. Or it might be a savory roast chicken. Fried chicken was reserved for times when Mama could be in the kitchen instead of in church.

Fried chicken was for suppers and picnics. Who ever had a picnic without a basket of fried chicken covered with a damask napkin? Broilers were a treat because most farmers preferred to keep their chickens until they had paid their way with new-laid eggs. Rock Cornish hens had not been invented, and I never heard of squab until I moved to Virginia. But we had plump, range-fed chickens raised in the good clean sun and not in wire cages.

Turkeys were for Thanksgiving and Christmas. They had plenty of dark meat, which has much more flavor, and they were stuffed with old-fashioned bread stuffing. It is convenient to be able to buy frozen turkey any time of year and nothing graces a buffet like a crisply browned turkey resting on a bed of watercress. But some of the magic has gone just because it is always around.

Duckling was scarce and goose was a rare treat. Wild game was plentiful and was shared with the neighbors. I have never been able to eat it, or venison either, although there is a fine moral distinction between eating a tame duckling and a wild duck.

There are, I imagine, hundreds of ways to prepare fowl, but I have my favorite recipes, and I never grow tired of chicken.

Chicken Cacciatore a la Stillmeadow

1 young roasting chicken, cut in pieces
1 beaten egg
  Flour
  Salt
  Pepper
  Basil
  Thyme
  Bacon fat or other cooking fat
1 20-oz. can tomatoes
1 tbsp. finely diced onion
  Grated Parmesan cheese

Roll chicken pieces in beaten egg and then in flour which has been seasoned with salt, pepper and a little basil and thyme. Brown in fat in a skillet. Place in an earthenware pot and pour tomatoes over the chicken. Add onion and stir in slightly. Top with a liberal amount of cheese and bake in a moderate oven for 1½ hours, or until the chicken is tender. Serves 4 to 6

If I were on a desert island and had only one thing to eat, I would undoubtedly choose chicken. I could survive on just chicken. Of course it would taste better cooked—as, for instance, Cacciatore.

Brunswick Stew

1 5-lb. stewing chicken, cut in pieces
¼ lb. salt pork, diced (or bacon)
  Salt, pepper
1 medium onion, diced
2 cups canned tomatoes (or four or five fresh, cut up
2½ cups green lima beans, fresh or frozen
3 potatoes, sliced thin
2½ cups canned or fresh corn
¼ lb. butter
4 tbsps. flour

Brown the chicken in the pork drippings, add a quart of water and simmer, covered, until the chicken is tender. (If you use your pressure cooker, follow directions for fricasseeing.) When chicken is tender, cool it enough to remove meat from the bones and cut in bite-sized pieces. Return to the kettle, add all the ingredients except corn and butter and flour. Cook until the vegetables are tender, then add corn and butter and cook about 5 minutes. Meanwhile blend about 4 tablespoons of flour with enough cold water to make a smooth mixture, and add to the stew to thicken it. Serves 8

I first had a variation of Brunswick Stew in Virginia and asked my hostess how it was made. "We just toss in whatever we have," she said vaguely. Some cooks add a can of condensed tomato soup; some, of course, add rabbit. It is company fare, served with a salad and hot biscuits.

Stillmeadow Fried Chicken

½ frying chicken for each person (you may use larger than usual for this method)
  Eggs, beaten lightly (1 egg to each fryer)
  Milk (1 tbsp. to an egg)
  Flour and seasoned bread crumbs (these come in a package), half of each (¾ cup to each fryer)
  Butter or margarine (2 tbsps. to each fryer)

Add the milk to the beaten eggs. Wipe the chicken with a clean damp cloth. Dip in the egg and milk. Dip in the flour and crumbs. Dip lightly again in the liquid to set the crumb mixture. Let rest while you heat the heavy skillet or electric frying pan with the butter or margarine. Dip again in the crumb and flour mix, and when the butter or margarine is bubbling hot (this is the best way I can describe it) lay the chicken pieces in.

Brown until golden, lift with tongs or a spatula (do not pierce with a fork and let those juices run out) turn and brown the other side. Then turn the heat low and continue to cook for 30 to 40 minutes. If the chicken shows signs of getting dry, cover the pan. Add a little salad oil if needed.

Serve on a hot platter, and I do mean hot.

This is a combination of Maryland fried chicken, Virginian fried chicken, and New England fried chicken. It is not according to any one rule. Also the covering is controversial. But it happens to work for me.

Gravy

For this, the chicken stays hot in the oven on a heat-proof platter. I stir in flour, 1 tablespoon, to 1 tablespoon of the drippngs and cracklings left in the pan. I then add the broth from having cooked the neck, the giblets, a bit of celery top, and a slice of onion. If this turns out to be short of liquid, I add thin cream or top milk. I do not let cream boil, this is fatal. But when it simmers and is ready to boil, the gravy is done.

Fried chicken and cream gravy such as this needs tiny hot biscuits (I use a mix) because a split biscuit takes so well to extra gravy.

Serve a non-starchy vegetable such as spinach or asparagus or broiled tomatoes with this, a very crisp green salad with nothing but oil and vinegar on the side. And who wants dessert? Just reach for one more bite of chicken.

I sometimes, when hurried, do the seasoned-flour version. I shake the chicken up in a paper bag, praying it won't have a hole in it, with plenty of flour, salt, pepper, paprika, a dash of onion salt. Then I proceed as above.

I could never approximate my Virginia cook's fried chicken, but then, I never got the recipe. She said she just fried it, being careful. But the Stillmeadow Fried Chicken never seems to have any leftovers, so I shall have to settle for that.

The Old Oaken Bucket

How dear to this heart are the scenes of my childhood,
  When fond recollection presents them to view!
The orchard, the meadow, the deep-tangled wildwood,
  And every loved spot which my infancy knew;
The wide-spreading pond, and the mill that stood by it;
  The bridge and the rock where the cataract fell;
The cot of my father, the dairy-house nigh it,
  And e'en the rude bucket which hung in the well!
The old oaken bucket, the iron-bound bucket,
  The moss-covered bucket which hung in the well.

That moss-covered vessel I hail as a treasure;
  For often, at noon, when returned from the field,
I found it the source of an exquisite pleasure,
  The purest and sweetest that nature can yield.
How ardent I seized it, with hands that were glowing,
  And quick to the white-pebbled bottom it fell;
Then soon, with the emblem of truth overflowing,
  And dripping with coolness, it rose from the well;
The old oaken bucket, the iron-bound bucket,
  The moss-covered bucket arose from the well.

How sweet from the green mossy brim to receive it,
  As poised on the curb, it inclined to my lips!
Not a full blushing goblet could tempt me to leave it,
  Though filled with the nectar which Jupiter sips;
And now, far removed from thy loved situation,
  The tear of regret will intrusively swell,
As fancy reverts to my father's plantation,
  And sighs for the bucket which hangs in the well;
The old oaken bucket, the iron-bound bucket,
  The moss-covered bucket, which hangs in the well.

Selected from "The Old Oaken Bucket"
Samuel Woodworth

Laura Ingalls Wilder: Stories That Had to Be Told

William Anderson

To Laura Ingalls Wilder, memories of life as a pioneer girl were "altogether too good to be lost." They were simply "stories that had to be told."

So, at sixty-five, Laura Wilder, a pretty, white-haired farm lady of Mansfield, Missouri, opened an orange-covered school tablet, intent upon writing a book. From her warm memories and from her heart, she spun tales that are now classics—stories of real people, in real places and the actual events that she herself saw as a wide-eyed pioneer girl of the 1870s and 1880s.

Not until she was seventy-six did Laura lay down her pencil—and only after she had written eight books—her own life story from the ages of five to eighteen, in what millions now know as the "Little House" stories.

Laura explained her reasons for writing thusly: "I wanted children now to understand more about the beginnings of things, to know what is behind the things they see, what it is that made America as they know it. I thought of writing . . . an eight-volume historical novel for children, covering every aspect of the American frontier. I had seen the whole frontier, the woods, the Indians of the great plains, the frontier town, the building of railroads, homesteading and farmers . . . I realized that I had seen it all—all the successive phases of the frontier: first the frontiersman, then the pioneer, then the farmer, then the towns. I understood that in my own life, I represented a period of American history. . . ."

Laura had indeed "seen it all"—all that made up America's great Expansionist days of the last century. She and her family played a part in pushing back the raw western territory, and one day, Laura's own gentle, flawless recall would make it seem alive again. As a girl along the western trail, she had stood on a dry-goods box, helping her mother at the camp-table; at night on the other side of the canvas wagon top, she heard wolves paw and howl. Drought, disease and dust storms had blown her way. Blizzards, fire and flood had taught her nature's force. She had watched the earth, angry at invasion, buckle against her father's turning plow.

Yet in Laura's memory, a graceful beauty—beauty born in strength—remained. Delicate wildflowers bloomed where wolves prowled, and billowing clouds brought gentle breezes, as well as blizzard blasts. The joy of living through hardship as a member of a close-knit family always welled up as the grown-up pioneer girl mused over her past. Laura Ingalls Wilder wanted to share.

When Laura Ingalls was born in 1867, western Wisconsin was still covered with deep woods. As a wise old woman, she remembered her birthplace and first home as **Little House in the Big Woods**. But more important than that gray log house were the people who lived there. With her Pa, Charles Ingalls, Laura felt a special kinship. "He was a trapper and frontiersman," his daughter said, "jolly, inclined to be reckless, and he loved his violin." Ma, Caroline Quiner Ingalls, balanced Pa's exhuberance. From a Boston family, Ma was cool and refined, her love of culture almost as strong as her love of family. "My parents exhibited the spirit of the pioneer to a marked degree," Laura stated. But it was Ma who always finalized matters with "whatever you say, Charles" or "you know best."

Among Laura's earliest memories were the family's first pioneering journey to Indian Territory, now Kansas. With wide-eyed anticipation Laura and sister Mary watched Pa load the prairie schooner, bound for the vast open spaces he longed for. In the Osage Indian Territory, days were busy with cabin building, crop planting and the day-to-day life Laura would one day record in **Little House on the Prairie**. But nighttimes held the sound of the Indian war whoop, which Laura never forgot. And when the Federal government told the Ingalls family and their scattered neighbors that they must leave the Red Man's land, they left. Once again Laura heard the swish of tall prairie grass against the wagon wheels. The wheels were rolling them north again.

When Pa stopped the wagon, they were still on the prairie, but on the flat farming lands of western Minnesota. **On the Banks of Plum Creek**, Pa and Ma set up home in a dugout. Closeby was the village of Walnut Grove, with a railroad running east and west. To Pa, that railroad meant a market for wheat. To Ma, the town meant school and church. Mary and Laura and little Carrie went to school. For the first time Laura knew, what she called, "the fascination of writing" and expressing the thoughts which lay within.

Many years later, Laura was asked about her writing skill. She had gone to "little red schoolhouses all over the west," she said, and "was never graduated from anything." But she credited her parents with her talent in expression. "The only reason I can think of being able to write at all was that father and mother were great readers and I read a lot at home with them."

Railroads were inching their tracks west into Dakota Territory, and once more Pa wanted to move. Grasshoppers and drought had ruined his plans for success in Minnesota. Disease had blinded beautiful Mary and a son had died, between the births of Carrie and Grace. Laura, at twelve, was her parents' stout helpmate and Mary's link to color and light. On the day when Mary saw no more, Laura began serving as her sister's eyes. That job was the apprenticeship to a storytelling career.

The Ingalls Home in DeSmet, South Dakota
Built by Pa Ingalls in 1887

One final move took the Ingalls family to DeSmet, Dakota Territory, where they became first settlers of the place Laura would call **Little Town on the Prairie**. They nearly starved there during the famous "hard winter" of 1880-1881, when blizzards shut off supplies and fuel for six months. Only wheat ground into coarse flour and hay twisted into sticks kept Laura and her family alive. "There is something," Laura observed "in living close to the great elemental forces of nature that causes people to rise above small annoyances and discomforts."

Continued

At eighteen, after teaching three terms of country school, Laura married Almanzo Wilder, the New York "farmer boy" who became a Dakota homesteader. Laura, independent and forthright, balked at the use of the word "obey" in their 1885 wedding service. "Almanzo," she explained, "even if I tried, I do not think I could obey anybody against my better judgment." Almanzo agreed.

As a team, the young Wilders set out to become successful South Dakota farmers. While the first stirrings of feminism were being felt, Laura Wilder was already her husband's equal partner on their prairie acres. With pride she told how "I learned to do all kinds of farm work with machinery. I have ridden the binder, driving six horses."

"No one," asserted Laura, "who has not homesteaded, can understand the fascination and the terror of it." The Wilders saw their house burn, their son die and a $3,000 wheat crop flatten under great sweeps of hail. Almanzo lost his health after a diphtheria attack and nearly everything else he owned by crop failure.

The burdens in South Dakota became too great. In 1894, the Wilders, with seven-year-old daughter Rose, left to begin a new life in the Ozark Mountains of Missouri. After a month of travel, they reached the hills that lured them. Driving through valleys and hollows, camping in the oak woods, drinking from the numberless springs, they were coming home. As the covered wagon pulled into Mansfield, Missouri, Laura said in a voice full of hope, "This is where we stop."

After a lifetime of journeying, Laura had found her homeplace among the blue hazy hills. She and Almanzo located a tract of wooded ridge land, with crazily angled ravines and soft-shouldered hills. They bought the place and Laura christened it Rocky Ridge Farm. On the land stood a windowless log cabin, where light filtered through the cracks in the walls. "So did the wind and rain," Laura laughed many years later.

Together, Laura and Almanzo cleared land, planted an orchard, raised crops and livestock. Laura tended poultry and grew locally famous for her methods and high egg yields. The farm grew to 200 acres, and from materials on their land, the Wilders built a ten-room country home.

Content in the peaceful vistas of Rocky Ridge, Laura found purpose in her role as farmwife. "We who live in quiet places," she wrote, "have the opportunity to become acquainted with ourselves, to think our own thoughts and live our own lives." She questioned women who rallied against the lives of housewives. "Farm women have always been wage earners and partners in their husbands' business," she pointed out. "It is rather amusing to read flaring headlines announcing the fact that women are at last coming into their own," she continued. "Farm women have always been business women, but no one has even noticed it."

A hardy frontierswoman and capable farmwife, Laura was also a refined intellectual. She founded a farm loan company, worked to better conditions for women in the Ozarks and accepted invitations to speak at public meetings. For a dozen years, she was Household Editor of the **Missouri Ruralist**, contributing homespun, but heartfelt, columns of her views of the world.

The Wilders' only child had become Rose Wilder Lane, indomitable journalist, author and world traveler. In 1915, while Rose was a celebrated San Francisco newspaper woman, she urged her mother to come west. Laura, eager to learn more about writing from her daughter, made the trip. But as she told Almanzo, she would not trade California "for one Ozark hill."

Not until 1930 did Laura Ingalls Wilder first try her hand at writing books for children. At Rose's request, she penciled a few childhood tales, and an interested publisher asked for a book. When **Little House in the Big Woods** appeared in 1932, the new author "thought that would end it." But publishers' pleas and children's begging letters encouraged her through the eleven years it took to complete her series.

As a popular author, Laura took her fame in a quiet, modest way. Libraries were named for her, writing awards were sent to her, but she preferred to think that all pioneers, not just herself, were being honored through her work. Letters filled the mailbox from far-off fans, and patiently the author answered each one. On her eighty-fourth birthday, 900 cards were delivered to her door. Strangers, people who had read the "Little House" books, were constantly stopping at Rocky Ridge to meet the Wilders. Laura said that summer tourists must outdo farmers in rising early; one family came knocking at seven in the morning.

When Almanzo, Laura's companion through sixty-four years of marriage, died in 1949, she was left lonely in the mellowing old farmhouse. But her days were filled with friends and letters and an active interest in the world around her. "Old age?" she asked, "There are things much more interesting to do than keeping tally of the years."

Once, toward the end of her long life, Laura was asked about the changes in living she had seen. "It seems impossible to me," she mused, "that I have seen so many changes in living, some good, some very wrong in my opinion. The old spirit of sturdy independence seems to be vanishing. We all depend too much on others. As modern life is lived, we have to do so, and more and more the individual alone is helpless. A conflict with nature and the elements is a clean fight, but a struggle against man and his contrivances is something very different. At times I have a homesick longing for the old days and the old ways. However, I know there is no turning back. We must go on."

Laura had made a graceful transition from one generation to another and in her own special way left behind a significant slice of the past. Before she died in 1957, at ninety, she had experienced miracles of technology: telephones, television, an airplane flight across the country. But as she told her youthful admirers, "The real things haven't changed."

"It is still best to be honest and truthful; to make the most of what we have; to be happy with simple pleasures and to be cheerful and have courage when things go wrong. Great improvements in living have been made because every American has always been free to pursue his happiness, and so long as Americans are free they will continue to make our country ever more wonderful."

The Prairie Is My Garden
by Harvey Dunn;
South Dakota Memorial Art Center Collection, Brookings

Shades of
Our Ancestors

Ruth B. Field

Itinerant artists of an olden day
Cut profiles from shadows on the wall
Of belles and beaux and children at play—
Dark silhouettes quite popular with all,
A regal lady's head with odd hairdo,
A gentleman with ruffles and coattails,
Maids with dolls, a ribbon curlicue,
A little lad holds close his boat with sails,
Parasols and fans, strange old hats—
Profiles cut with skill and greatest care—
Pompous men with ludicrous cravats,
For small details the cutter had a flair.
Family groups or a dignitary's head,
Dainty miss in lacy pantalets,
Though cutters and their art are long since fled,
We treasure still their quaint old silhouettes.

A Little Bit of Eden

As written in the Bible, God created man and woman and placed them in an ideal environment, the beautiful Garden of Eden, containing numerous beautiful and useful plants and the full range of wild but docile animals. In this harmonious, peaceful bit of heaven on earth, they enjoyed themselves in caring for the Garden and walking and conversing with God (Genesis 1).

Because of the perverse nature of man, the Garden of Eden was lost, and the harmony of the world was gone forever. But did we lose everything? Absolutely not! The world that God created was not destroyed but altered, no longer operating in the manner once intended. The parts are still here to be enjoyed and to be of use to mankind.

Observe that as the seasons progress through the year, there is an amazing array of blooms from trees, shrubs and wild flowers. The continuous succession of bloom unfolds like a magic carpet. Observe how tiny seeds amazingly produce many kinds of plants including large herbs, shrubs and trees. Observe the astounding variation in plant forms from mosses to ferns, to grasses, to flowering plants, and many others. Observe the glorious changing seasons that constantly repeat themselves. A little bit of Eden is very evident in our land.

A great number of plants have adapted themselves to many different environments from mountain to plain, from wetland to desert, from subtropics to the northland. In each plant community is found a uniquely different combination of animals which have adapted to their specific environment. Both the plants and the animals reveal the constant evolutionary processes that have given us many more kinds of life. The evolutionary process is a creative mechanism that has continued to enrich our earth. Bits of Eden have been expanding.

If a section of land is cleared and left undisturbed, the earth soon develops a great variety of plants. Many of these are weeds that temporarily help to protect the soil. Soon they are replaced by more permanent grasses and flowering plants, and later by shrubs and trees. The ragweeds that produced much of the hay fever will have disappeared, being replaced by more beautiful and useful plants. Parts of Eden often readily reappear on our land.

The variety and the beauty of the plants that are descendants from the Garden of Eden have been a pleasure to millions of people who flock from urban areas to the countryside. Like Adam and Eve, people still like to walk (or run or ride) where bits of Eden exist.

Because of neglect, ignorance or greed, our plant varieties are disappearing at a rate of at least one per week. The earth is turning from a garden into a waste dump and an asphalt desert at a slow but persistent rate. Our inheritance from Eden is slipping away.

What can be done to preserve our national heritage of flora, fauna and beautiful scenery? There are no easy answers, but there are solutions. Certainly, the helter-skelter building of houses, roads, parking lots, and many other structures can be more wisely controlled to protect our existing lands and scenic areas. Why should structures be built without requiring consideration of unique or valuable land features and requiring a degree of open planted areas? As is being done in a few states, why can't our roadsides and access areas be planted with native vegetation, thereby preserving and beautifying our countryside? Why do weed controllers persist in cutting down native vegetation under the guise of controlling weeds? The process is costly, creates ugly areas and actually encourages the very weeds they wish to eliminate. Native perennials have practically no hay fever-producing pollen. Why should there be so much indiscriminate dumping of wastes? Shouldn't all dumping be regulated to prevent further destruction of our heritage? The results of poor regulations have caused losses in our environment that far exceed any gains that have been made materially or aesthetically.

Those of us who love this country should have the foresight and courage to fight to keep a little of Eden in our land. We are a long way from the Garden of Adam and Eve, but there is much more to life than the gross national product.

Harold W. Rock

In God's Great Out-of-Doors

Out in the sunny pastures,
  The herds of cattle graze.
Up in the highest treetops,
  The birds sing songs of praise.
Far over cliffs so rocky,
  The kingly eagle soars,
And all are joyous, living
  In God's great out-of-doors.

In dense and shady forests,
  Wild creatures work and play,
And there the little squirrel
  Is busy all the day.
Deep in the hollow tree trunks,
  A pile of nuts, he stores,
For he must live all winter
  In God's great out-of-doors.

Above the country village,
  The smoke from chimneys curls,
And playing in the dooryards,
  Are merry boys and girls.
From morning until evening,
  The farmer toils and chores,
But he is hale, from living
  In God's great out-of-doors.

These homely country pictures
  Hold many charms for me.
I love the brooklet's music,
  And the ever restless sea
Just seems to loudly call me,
  With a voice that fairly roars,
And urges me to tarry
  In God's great out-of-doors.

How wonderful is nature!
  How promising the thought
That everything created,
  By God's own hand was wrought;
And not just here about us,
  But far on distant shores,
His vigilance encircles
  All His great out-of-doors.

Agnes Davenport Bond

They Walked Here

The "Kissing Bridge" they call it.
Quiet Sundays and fragrant summer nights
Echoed with lighthearted laughter,
heard the dreams and promises
of long-ago lovers.
This dim secluded meeting place played
a part in many romantic ecstasies,
And no lover failed to steal a kiss when
horse and buggy passed beneath its cover.

They walked here in this gloom
where water gurgles
beneath the old plank floor
That once knew the harsh gashings of
wagon wheel and horse's hoof,
The burning, sparking slide of heavy
sleigh runners on the dry and sturdy planking,
The hobnailed boots of weary travelers
who sought protection beneath its roof.

It was here the night traveler, blinded
by endless black, fell to the robber.
Here too, men sought safety from cruelty
of storm to await the breaking of the day.
Bears lumbered through this cavern;
wildcats crouched on the rafters,
nursing their cunning,
Hungry for the victims forced to brave
the lonely desolate trail this way.

Here, too, stalked grim disaster and
tragedy in springtime and autumn flood,
When raging water clawed the foundation
loose and split apart the seams,
Dragging the quivering structure down
into the roaring, rioting waters;
But come fair weather, again those
pioneers wearily bridged the stream.

They walked here, those old pioneers,
over this creaking covered bridge
Where dust grows thicker and thicker
as time goes flying by;
Dust that corrodes the aged
and battered rough-log timbers,
And blackens each seasoned criss-cross
beam and chiseled tie.

Recorded here on the mighty arches, the
great timbers shaped by hand,
Are the carvings and signatures
of travelers and yesteryear's friends;
And here, quaintly artistic,
are roughlined heart pictures
with scraggly initials,
Mute pledges to the kind of sweet friendship
that has no foreseeable end.

What memories it could relate to those
who walk here now in wonderment;
What stories it holds away from those
who reverence its construction and atmosphere.
But all is silent, no rumbling carriage
wheels, no horse's brisk clip-clopping pace,

No sweet youthful laughter, or hearty
voices of pioneers.
All is quiet, but we know they walked here.

Helen Shick

A Chapter of Americana
The Adventures
of
Tom Sawyer
Mark Twain

Tom's mind was made up now. He was gloomy and desperate. He was a forsaken, friendless boy, he said; nobody loved him; when they found out what they had driven him to, perhaps they would be sorry; he had tried to do right and get along, but they would not let him; since nothing would do them but to be rid of him, let it be so; and let them blame him for the consequences—why shouldn't they? What right had the friendless to complain? Yes, they had forced him to it at last: he would lead a life of crime. There was no choice.

By this time he was far down Meadow Lane, and the bell of school to "take up" tinkled faintly upon his ear. He sobbed, now, to think he should never, never hear that old familiar sound any more—it was very hard, but it was forced on him; since he was driven out into the cold world, he must submit—but he forgave them. Then the sobs came thick and fast.

Just at this point he met his soul's sworn comrade, Joe Harper—hard-eyed, and with evidently a great and dismal purpose in his heart. Plainly here were "two souls with but a single thought." Tom, wiping his eyes with his sleeve, began to blubber out something about a resolution to escape from hard usage and lack of sympathy at home by roaming abroad into the great world never to return, and ended by hoping that Joe would not forget him.

But it transpired that this was a request which Joe had just been going to make of Tom, and had come to hunt him up for that purpose. His mother had whipped him for drinking some cream which he had never tasted and knew nothing about; it was plain that she was tired of him and wished him to go; if she felt that way, there was nothing for him to do but succumb; he hoped she would be happy and never regret having driven her poor boy out into the unfeeling world to suffer and die.

As the two boys walked sorrowing along, they made a new compact to stand by each other and be brothers and never separate till death relieved them of their troubles. Then they began to lay their plans. Joe was for being a hermit, and living on crusts in a remote cave, and dying, some time, of cold and want and grief; but after listening to Tom, he conceded that there were some conspicuous advantages about a life of crime, and so he consented to be a pirate.

Three miles below St. Petersburg, at a point where the Mississippi River was a trifle over a mile wide, there was a long, narrow, wooded island, with a shallow bar at the head of it, and this offered well as a rendezvous. It was not inhabited; it lay far over toward the further shore, abreast a dense and almost wholly unpeopled forest. So Jackson's Island was chosen. Who were to be the subjects of their piracies, was a matter that did not occur to them. Then they hunted up Huckleberry Finn, and he joined them promptly, for all careers were one to him; he was indifferent. They presently separated to meet at a lonely spot on the riverbank two miles above the village at the favorite hour—which was midnight. There was a small log raft there which they meant to capture. Each would bring hooks and lines, and such provision as he could steal in the most dark and mysterious way—as became outlaws. And before the afternoon was done, they had all managed to enjoy the sweet glory of spreading the fact that pretty soon the town would "hear something." All who got this vague hint were cautioned to "be mum and wait."

About midnight Tom arrived with a boiled ham and a few trifles, and stopped in a dense undergrowth on a small bluff overlooking the meeting-place. It was starlight, and very still. The mighty river lay like an ocean at rest. Tom listened a moment, but no sound disturbed the quiet. Then he gave a low, distinct whistle. It was answered from under the bluff. Tom whistled twice more; these signals were answered in the same way. Then a guarded voice said:

"Who goes there?"

"Tom Sawyer, the Black Avenger of the Spanish Main. Name your names."

"Huck Finn the Red-Handed, and Joe Harper the Terror of the Seas." Tom had furnished these titles, from his favorite literature.

"'Tis well. Give the countersign."

Two hoarse whispers delivered the same awful word simultaneously to the brooding night:

"BLOOD!"

Then Tom tumbled his ham over the bluff and let himself down after it, tearing both skin and clothes to some extent in the effort. There was an easy, comfortable path along the shore under the bluff, but it lacked the advantages of difficulty and danger so valued by a pirate.

The Terror of the Seas had brought a side of bacon, and had about worn himself out with getting it there. Finn the Red-Handed had stolen a skillet and a quantity of half-cured leaf tobacco, and had also brought a few corncobs to make pipes with. But none of the pirates smoked or chewed but himself. The Black Avenger of the Spanish Main said it would never do to start without some fire. That was a wise thought; matches were hardly known there in that day. They saw a fire smoldering upon a great raft a hundred yards above, and they went stealthily thither and helped themselves to a chunk. They made an imposing adventure of it, saying, "Hist!" every now and then, and suddenly halting with finger on lip; moving with hands on imaginary dagger-hilts; and giving orders in dismal whispers that if "the foe" stirred, to "let him have it to the hilt," because "dead men tell no tales." They knew well enough that the raftsmen were all down at the village laying in stores or having a spree, but still that was no excuse for their conducting this thing in an unpiratical way.

They shoved off, presently, Tom in command, Huck at the after oar and Joe at the forward. Tom stood amidships, gloomy-browed, and with folded arms, and gave his orders in a low, stern whisper:

"Luff, and bring her to the wind!"

"Aye-aye, sir!"

"Steady, steady-y-y-y!"

"Steady it is, sir!"

"Let her go off a point!"

"Point it is, sir!"

As the boys steadily and monotonously drove the raft toward midstream it was no doubt understood that these orders were given only for "style," and were not intended to mean anything in particular.

"What sail's she carrying?"

"Courses, tops'ls, and flying-jib, sir."

"Send the r'yals up! Lay out aloft, there, half a dozen of ye—foretopmaststuns'l! Lively, now!"

"Aye-aye, sir!"

"Shake out that maintogalans'l! Sheets and braces! **Now**, my hearties!"

"Aye-aye, sir!"

"Hellum-a-lee—hard a port! Stand by to meet her when she comes! Port, port! **Now**, men! With a will! Stead-y-y-y!"

"Steady it is, sir!"

The raft drew beyond the middle of the river; the boys pointed her head right, and then lay on their oars. The river was not high, so there was not more than a two or

three mile current. Hardly a word was said during the next three-quarters of an hour. Now the raft was passing before the distant town. Two or three glimmering lights showed where it lay, peacefully sleeping, beyond the vague vast sweep of star-gemmed water, unconscious of the tremendous event that was happening. The Black Avenger stood still with folded arms, "looking his last" upon the scene of his former joys and his later sufferings, and wishing "she" could see him now, abroad on the wild sea, facing peril and death with dauntless heart, going to his doom with a grim smile on his lips. It was but a small strain on his imagination to remove Jackson's Island beyond eyeshot of the village, and so he "looked his last" with a broken and satisfied heart. The other pirates were looking their last, too; and they all looked so long that they came near letting the current drift them out of the range of the island. But they discovered the danger in time, and made shift to avert it. About two o'clock in the morning the raft grounded on the bar two hundred yards above the head of the island, and they waded back and forth until they had landed their freight. Part of the little raft's belongings consisted of an old sail, and this they

Continued

spread over a nook in the bushes for a tent to shelter their provisions; but they themselves would sleep in the open air in good weather, as became outlaws.

They built a fire against the side of a great log twenty or thirty steps within the somber depths of the forest, and then cooked some bacon in the frying pan for supper, and used up half of the corn pone stock they had brought. It seemed glorious sport to be feasting in that wild free way in the virgin forest of an unexplored and uninhabited island, far from the haunts of men, and they said they never would return to civilization. The climbing fire lit up their faces and threw its ruddy glare upon the pillared tree trunks of their forest temple, and upon the varnished foliage and festooning vines.

When the last crisp slice of bacon was gone, and the last allowance of corn pone devoured, the boys stretched themselves out on the grass, filled with contentment. They could have found a cooler place, but they would not deny themselves such a romantic feature as the roasting camp-fire.

"**Ain't** it gay?" said Joe.

"It's **nuts!**" said Tom. "What would the boys say if they could see us?"

"Say? Well, they'd just die to be here—hey, Hucky!"

"I reckon so," said Huckleberry, "anyways, I'm suited. I don't want nothing better'n this. I don't ever get enough to eat, gen'ally—and here they can't come and pick at a feller and bullyrag him so."

"It's just the life for me," said Tom. "You don't have to get up mornings, and you don't have to go to school, and wash, and all that blame foolishness. You see a pirate don't have to **anything**, Joe, when he's ashore; but a hermit **he** has to be praying considerable, and then he don't have any fun, anyway, all by himself that way."

"Oh, yes, that's so," said Joe, "but I hadn't thought much about it, you know. I'd a good deal rather be a pirate, now that I've tried it."

"You see," said Tom, "people don't go much on hermits, nowadays, like they used to in old times, but a pirate's always respected. And a hermit's got to sleep on the hardest place he can find, and put sackcloth and ashes on his head, and stand out in the rain, and—"

"What does he put sackcloth and ashes on his head for?" inquired Huck.

"I dunno. But they've **got** to do it. Hermits always do. You'd have to do that if you was a hermit."

"Dern'd if I would," said Huck.

"Well, what would you do?"

"I dunno. But I wouldn't do that."

"Why, Huck, you'd **have** to. How'd you get around it?"

"Why, I just wouldn't stand it. I'd run away."

"Run away! Well, you **would** be a nice old slouch of a hermit. You'd be a disgrace."

The Red-Handed made no response, being better employed. He had finished gouging out a cob, and now he fitted a weed stem to it, loaded it with tobacco, and was pressing a coal to the charge and blowing a cloud of fragrant smoke—he was in the full bloom of luxurious contentment. The other pirates envied him this majestic vice and secretly resolved to acquire it shortly. Presently Huck said:

"What does pirates have to do?" Tom said: "Oh, they have just a bully time—take ships and burn them, and get the money and bury it in awful places in their island where there's ghosts and things to watch it, and kill everybody in the ships—make 'em walk a plank."

"And they carry the women to the island," said Joe; "they don't kill the women."

"No," assented Tom, "they don't kill the women—they're too noble. And the women's always beautiful, too."

"And don't they wear the bulliest clothes! Oh, no! All gold and silver and di'monds," said Joe, with enthusiasm.

"Who?" said Huck.

"Why, the pirates."

Huck scanned his own clothing forlornly.

"I reckon I ain't dressed fitten for a pirate," said he, with a regretful pathos in his voice, "but I ain't got none but these."

But the other boys told him the fine clothes would come fast enough, after they should have begun their adventures. They made him understand that his poor rags would do to begin with, though it was customary for wealthy pirates to start with a proper wardrobe.

Gradually their talk died out and drowsiness began to steal upon the eyelids of the little waifs. The pipe dropped from the fingers of the Red-Handed, and he slept the sleep of the conscience-free and the weary. The Terror of the Seas and the Black Avenger of the Spanish Main had more difficulty in getting to sleep. They said their prayers inwardly, and lying down, since there was nobody there with authority to make them kneel and recite aloud; in truth, they had a mind not to say them at all, but they were afraid to proceed to such lengths as that, lest they might call down a sudden and special thunderbolt from Heaven. Then at once they reached and hovered upon the imminent verge of sleep—but an intruder came, now, that would not "down." It was conscience. They began to feel a vague fear that they had been doing wrong to run away; and next they thought of the stolen meat, and then the real torture came. They tried to argue it away by reminding conscience that they had purloined sweetmeats and apples scores of times; but conscience was not to be appeased by such thin plausibilities; it seemed to them, in the end, that there was no getting around the stubborn fact that taking sweetmeats was only "hooking," while taking bacon and hams and such valuables was plain simple **stealing**—and there was a command against that in the Bible. So they inwardly resolved that so long as they remained in the business, their piracies should not again be sullied with the crime of stealing. Then conscience granted a truce, and these curiously inconsistent pirates fell peacefully to sleep.

Out Where the West Begins

Arthur Chapman

Out where the handclasp's a little stronger,
Out where the smile dwells a little longer,
That's where the West begins;
Out where the sun is a little brighter,
Where the snows that fall are a trifle whiter,
Where the bonds of home are a wee bit tighter,
That's where the West begins.

From OUT WHERE THE WEST BEGINS by Arthur Chapman.
Copyright renewed 1945 by Kathleen C. Chapman. Reprinted
by permission of Houghton Mifflin Company.

Out where the skies are a trifle bluer,
Out where friendship's a little truer,
   That's where the West begins;
      Out where a fresher breeze is blowing,
      Where there's laughter in every streamlet flowing,
      Where there's more of reaping and less of sowing,
         That's where the West begins.

      Out where the world is in the making,
      Where fewer hearts in despair are aching,
         That's where the West begins;
            Where there's more of singing and less of sighing,
            Where there's more of giving and less of buying,
            And a man makes friends without half trying—
               That's where the West begins.

A Lesson in July

Calm weather, warm breezes, blue skies,
And bright sunshine,
All put together were a day in July.
They drew me to the place where the water
Meets the sand and told me that now
I was resting in God's hand.

A warm boulder was my chair.
I sat relaxed, sensing life, unaware,
Feeling neither joy or strife.
Just being was enough for time and place.
Awareness came when a sound stirred my mind,
To see a truth, small but great,
Acted out right at my feet.
I saw the little ripples charge the shore

And laughed at their futile efforts,
Until I saw that the rock was worn
By their relentless beat. Each time
They seemed to retreat, I saw, they only fell back
To regroup. Each new charge came in bigger waves,
With greater force, until they washed
The shoreline out of sight.

John Fred Schilling

The Sea

Oh, take me back to the sea again,
To the sound of the waves that beat.
Let me run through the rush of the pounding surf
And feel the sand neath my feet.

Let me lay with my face upturned to the sky,
While watching the sea gulls soar.
Let my ears hear the peaceful silence
Of all but the waves that roar.

Let me lift my eyes to the sky above
And stretch in the warming sun.
Let me look to far horizons
Where sea and sky are one.

Let me gaze out across the water,
As the golden sun sets in the west.
Let my thoughts drift on to another day
As I close my eyes in rest.

Oh, take me back to the sea again,
To the beautiful, beautiful sea,
Where I can live on endless dreams
And memories that never flee.

Patricia A. Brown

North Woods Notebook
Pass the Whipped Cream!

My husband, Bob, was the youngest of ten children born to Comb and Anna Andersen Bourgeois. The family lived in Park Falls, Wisconsin, when Bob was born on August 20, 1923; during his childhood there were several moves to farms and small towns throughout northern Wisconsin.

Bob's memories of his childhood remain vivid. When he talks about those distant days, the memories come alive; they are echoes of a way of life that has all but disappeared from the American scene.

It's a wonder I can still look a strawberry straight in the eye! I must have picked millions of them in the summers of my childhood, bending over under the hot sun to earn the princely sum of two cents per quart. There were not many paying jobs for kids in those days, so every one of us put in time in the strawberry patch. We probably ate two berries for every ten that we picked, but our real motive was income—cash on hand for the Fourth of July carnival.

Every year there was a Strawberry Festival in Bayfield on the Fourth of July. The Women's Auxiliary of the American Legion would set up a tent where they served nothing but strawberry shortcake—homemade cake, fresh berries, and fresh whipped cream. It cost a quarter to get in, and then you could have all the strawberry shortcake you wanted. To me it was sheer heaven, although I recall that more than once I left that tent with a powerful feeling of nausea.

Dad just loved the Fourth of July. He always saw to it that there were plenty of firecrackers on hand, the louder the better. Dad would get up very early, about five o'clock, and he would set off several loud bombs to start the celebrating. The kids in the neighborhood loved all the excitement, and the neighbors never complained, but our dog nearly went crazy. He would hide under my bed for the entire day and night; maybe he thought the world was coming to an end, or maybe the sharp explosions hurt his ears. Anyway, we never saw the dog again until July fifth.

I remember how proud Dad was of the medals he had earned during his service in the Spanish-American War. Every Fourth of July he would get them out of the box in his dresser and pin them all on his best white shirt.

There was always a picnic around the Fourth of July, even though it took some incredible planning to get us all together. All my brothers and sisters came, even the married ones, and everybody brought carloads of food. Sometimes we picnicked on the shore of Lake Superior and sometimes at a small, inland lake or on a river bank.

My brothers and I did a lot of trout fishing during the summer, whenever we weren't lined up for farm chores. Our favorite spots were the streams that empty into Lake Superior, and if we were really lucky we'd bring home enough rainbow, brook, or German browns for our family dinner.

Sometimes Ed, Milt, and I would go fishing early in the morning. If the fish were biting and we caught our limit, we'd fix a shore lunch. After we cleaned the fish, we would wrap them in maple leaves and then in red clay. One of us would build a fire and we baked the fish until they were succulent, steaming, and delicious.

It could be that we enjoyed fishing so much because we had so little time for it. There was a lot of work to be done on the farm in the summer, and we all had to do our share. Sometimes I used to think that "summer" and "haying" were pretty much the same thing. Our hay crop had to be mowed, raked, stacked, and hauled to the barn. It was hot, dusty work and it was also physically exhausting. Everything was done by hand; the hay was not rolled or baled as it is nowadays.

Once the hay was mowed, it had to dry, so we stacked it into long rows across the field. Then we made hayshocks out of the rows, building them so that the rain would run off. We continually worried that it would rain before we could get the hay into the barn.

The hayshocks were always small enough so that two people could lift them with pitchforks onto the hay wagon. My brothers and I always competed with one another to see which one of us was strong enough to lift a hayshock all by himself. Our shoulder muscles ached, but it was a matter of honor to try and accomplish that feat of sheer strength.

Unfortunately, the hayshocks were ideal hiding places for snakes and mice. You never knew when a mouse would run down your arm, or when a snake would drop out of the hay and slither across your foot. The mice never bothered me, but I had a strong aversion to snakes and I was scared to death every time one popped out of the hay.

Once the hay arrived at the barn, someone had to stay inside the barn and keep moving the hay toward the back to make room for more. As the youngest child, I inherited that less than pleasant job. While the others got to work outdoors, I was stuck in that smelly barn where the temperature must have stayed well over 100 degrees. The hay was dry and dusty and prickly, and my arms and face were covered with sweat. Never

did a glass of lemonade taste as wonderful as it did when I finally got out of that barn!

My brothers and I spent hours every summer tramping through the woods looking for berries. We would take some of Ma's berry baskets or a couple old pails along and try to fill them with blueberries and blackberries, chokecherries or pin cherries. And although we tried to be very nonchalant, every one of us was terrified that we'd come eyeball to eyeball with a foraging bear who was also in the market for some fresh fruit.

Some of our courage went into every jar of jam that Ma ever made. And some of our back strain went into every piece of strawberry shortcake we devoured. Even so, my favorite dessert remains, to this day, strawberry shortcake.

Bea Bourgeois

Little Churches

Martha S. Hood

From Portland west to Portland,
From Duluth to the Rio Grande,
Safe only in America
Do little churches stand;
Of every thought and sect and creed,
The soul of freedom's there,
With every spire a guidepost,
And every stone a prayer.

They say—
"We are God's little churches,
Scattered wide o'er hill and dell,
In hamlet, field and forest
And on the seacoast far,
Wherever earnest, humble folk,
And quiet spirits dwell.
'Tis there we stand as witnesses
That here His children are.

"We seem to be so very small,
And weak, and scattered wide;
Yet there is one thing for Thee, Lord,
We all must surely do,
When travelers' roving eyes
Glance o'er the countryside,
They see us standing there and think of You.
And oh, our Father, there is need today
Of thoughts of You,
So keep us here, we pray.

"Our walls were raised by men of honest heart,
Who learned God's precepts and obeyed His law,
Who felt themselves of His great plan a part,
And knew that naught could last did He withdraw.
Now, though they slumber in their quiet rest,
Surely their works have followed them and proved
Their children strong to seize and hold the best,
And through life's wild confusion not be moved.
Beneath Thy soft wings' shadows let us hide
That, being true, we may with Thee abide."

And so—
From Portland west to Portland,
From Duluth to the Rio Grande,
Safe always in America
May little churches stand;
Of every faith and sect and creed,
The soul of freedom's there,
With every spire a guidepost,
And every stone a prayer.

I Love a Country Road

Garnett Ann Schultz

I love a quiet country road
That winds around the hill,
Where I can walk on summer days
When all is calm and still,
With pleasant fields on either side
Where cattle feed and graze.
There's nothing quite as magical
As wondrous country ways.

My heart would walk a country road
Where trees there offer shade,
A road that leads to valleys deep,
A pleasant little glade,
While shadows in the afternoon
Reach out like gentle arms,
And singing birds and buzzing bees
Add extra thrills and charms.

A winding road that climbs so high
Atop a summer hill,
Where breezes gently blow and play
Within the peace and still,
Somehow my cares then quickly fade
As I forget life's load,
For dreams then fill my heart and mind.
I love a country road.

Theodore Roosevelt, our twenty-sixth president, was everybody's hero. He was a refreshing personality and a leader who was unafraid to act or speak his mind. Ebullient, enthusiastic, vigorous, he was an inveterate traveler, a fighter, a hunter, a doting parent and adoring husband. Small wonder that, almost a century later, "Teddy" Roosevelt remains beloved.

Theodore Roosevelt's home, Sagamore Hill, in Oyster Bay, New York, brings to life his interests, his exuberant family, his hospitality at the informal, twenty-three-room Victorian frame and brick house. From the andirons made of shells and cannon balls to the buffalo head, it is all "Teddy Roosevelt."

Sagamore Hill, built by Roosevelt in 1885, perches on a hill that overlooks Oyster Cove, a vista the family enjoyed during long summer days and evenings on the deep, shaded piazza. The piazza was also where Colonel Roosevelt was welcomed home as a national hero of the Cuban war. He was later to become governor of New York, then, vice-president of the United States and, in 1904, president.

The fact is, every room in the spacious, sprawling house is a Roosevelt story unto itself, a reflection of outgoing personalities and an intimate look at beloved possessions. Typically,

Sagamore Hill

Mildred Jailer

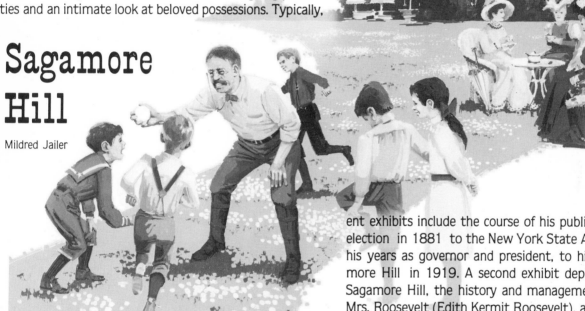

place for twenty to thirty experts, who came from around the country to discuss national issues and political strategies, and a reception room for the Roosevelts' formal entertaining. Here, too, there are curios, trophies and precious belongings: elk and deer antlers, the presidential flag, Roosevelt's Rough Riders sword, hat and revolver.

And so it goes throughout each of the colorful rooms of Sagamore Hill: the Red Bathroom at the top of the stairs which holds a huge porcelain bathtub, that the children called "sarcophagus," the landing with its huge rhinoceros, and the pantry that was equipped with a wall telephone during Roosevelt's presidency.

The Georgian home built in 1938 for General Theodore Roosevelt, Jr. in a former orchard on the Sagamore Hill property, is now The Old Orchard Museum. It is devoted to the many aspects of Theodore Roosevelt's life. The permanent exhibits include the course of his public career, from his election in 1881 to the New York State Assembly through his years as governor and president, to his death at Sagamore Hill in 1919. A second exhibit depicts family life at Sagamore Hill, the history and management of the estate, Mrs. Roosevelt (Edith Kermit Roosevelt), and Sagamore Hill as the "Summer White House." The third permanent exhibit is dedicated to the six Roosevelt children: Alice, Theodore, Jr., Kermit, Ethel, Archibald and Quentin.

A variety of film programs, featuring biographical films, recent television documentaries and some old silents, are shown at the museum. In addition, a small library is also maintained there.

the library is where, in 1905, Roosevelt met separately with the envoys of warring Russia and Japan before bringing them together for the conference that ended in the Treaty of Portsmouth. And it is where, during World War I, he spent evening after evening writing to his four sons in France. The library also contains a clock that chimes on the quarter hour, called the "ting tang clock" by the children, and a portrait of Theodore Roosevelt's father.

The mantelpiece in the master bedroom was the traditional hanging place for the Roosevelt children's Christmas stockings. The room has massive furniture bought by President Roosevelt's father at the 1876 Centennial Exposition in Philadelphia, where it had received an award for design. The thirty by forty-foot, wood-paneled North Room, added to the house in 1905, played a role similar to today's family room for that rough and tumble, close-knit family. The North Room also served more serious purposes: a meeting

Sagamore Hill is located three miles east of Oyster Bay on Long Island, close to the exclusive Long Island North Shore. About an hour-and-a-half drive from Sagamore Hill is the Theodore Roosevelt Birthplace on East 20th Street in New York City. A brownstone rowhouse similar to countless others of the mid-nineteenth century, it is furnished in formal, lavishly decorated style. The family moved to a larger home when Theodore was fourteen years old.

Both Sagamore Hill and the Theodore Roosevelt Birthplace are National Historic Sites, well worth visiting for the glimpse they afford into the life of this famous American.

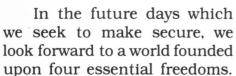

THE FOUR FREEDOMS

In the future days which we seek to make secure, we look forward to a world founded upon four essential freedoms.

The first is freedom of speech and expression—everywhere in the world.

The second is freedom of every person to worship God in his own way—everywhere in the world.

The third is freedom from want, which, translated into world terms, means economic understanding which will secure to every nation a healthy peacetime life for its inhabitants—everywhere in the world.

The fourth is freedom from fear, which, translated into world terms, means a world-wide reduction of armaments to such a point and in such a thorough fashion that no nation will be in a position to commit an act of physical aggression against any neighbor—anywhere in the world.

Franklin Delano Roosevelt
January 6, 1941
From an address to Congress

Liberty's Prayer

Lord God of low tides and high hopes,
who has brought millions to our shores,
grant that each of them shall find the freedom he sailed for
in this land which honors
all who honor it.

Lord God of willing hands and opportunity,
of past failures, present mistakes and future successes,
who has brought man from wagon train to space capsule
and filled this great country,
imperfect though it may be called by some,
give equal dignity to all
and send word back to Thomas Jefferson
that we do try to fulfill the promises
he filed under the Declaration of Independence.

Lord God of foreign ancestors and homegrown Americans,
who taught strangers to live together,
do as much now for friends.
Remind fiery young hearts
that passion works best when tempered with reason
and that nothing was ever built up
and torn down at the same time.

Lord God of broken promises and hungry hearts
remind us constantly the land we call home wasn't built in a day,
bear with our failures, forgive us our trespasses.
As you once trained lightning and fireflies to live together,
teach us now that good intentions are a beginning not an end,
that doing is still better than hoping and wishing,
that today holds the cure of yesterday
and the torch I hold high
is Liberty's nightlight welcoming tomorrow
with a rainbow of freedom
rising from the thunder of despair.

Paul W. Keyes

All About Bubble Gum

William Childress

"The way you tell a real great kid,
The way you tell a chum,
Is after he's chewed it for a while,
You get his bubble gum."

Alas, history failed to record the name of the poet who wrote these noble lines. But he was obviously an expert observer of two phenomena: kids and bubble gum—with maybe some penny candy thrown in. The only real bubble-gum experts are kids; the two have gone together since 1906, when "the gum that blew up" first appeared on the American scene.

In the days of my own childhood we were loyal to only one bubble gum: Fleers—tough, chewy pink stuff that came wrapped as "kisses" with twisted paper tails. When you untwisted them, out popped the Fleers Dubble Bubble Kids.

Only in the direst emergencies would we opt for Brand X, usually a gumball dispensed by machine. It was small and cost a penny when a penny was a fortune. And it wasn't as durable as the delicious pink stuff. It did blow bubbles, of course, and still does, even though last year's sugar shortage nearly ended penny candy and gum in America. We might have had a pint-sized revolution if kids had only known about an even grimmer crisis. It had to do with the oil shortage; since petroleum is one base for gum, its shortage almost finished the job that a lack of sugar had started. ... But now let's go back to the fun!

Remember the furious bubble-blowing contests held in schoolyards in the '40s? I do. There was "Puff" McAdder (name changed because he's now a politician and I don't want to give him a free plug!) who blew a bubble as big as a beach ball. Even I, the school pygmy, achieved bubbles of basketball proportions, only to be vanquished by blowhards who almost certainly practiced in their sleep.

Teachers responsible for our well-being—read "neatness"—threw their hands up in horror after those gummy games when we entered classrooms latex-laden, mostly on our faces. And what could be more wonderful than chasing a pack of screaming girls while holding a pink and well-chewed wad ready to stick in their hair?

Pennies weren't from heaven in those days either, so cadging grew to a fine art. Most of us know dozens of ways, not all of them sanitary, to scavenge a free chew. First, and least desirable, was the direct approach, which soon taught us a thing or two about friendship. A so-so friend would hem and haw and maybe give you a chaw. An enemy would laugh—and maybe punch you—in your face. A really good friend would take his wad out of his mouth while it still had some sugar in it and allow you a few blissful chews before reclaiming it!

And did we come up with unbelievable storage places! Under the table (done surreptitiously at suppertime when parents weren't looking). Snugged against door moldings. Stuck to bed rails. Wedged behind our ears—the list is endless.

If you want someone to blame for this terrible vice, blame the ancient Greeks. They weren't forever blowing bubbles, but they chewed gum—or at least a substance called *mastiche* (Greek for "to chew") that came from the resin of a tree. A physician named Dioscorides even claimed it had curative powers.

By A.D. 200 the Mayans were at it too, chomping the coagulated juice of the sapodilla tree; the stuff later became known as chicle. The Mayans disappeared, but their descendants kept chicle-chewing alive well into the 19th century.

American Indians had spruce gum. And as a kid on a Texas farm I chewed "sweet gum," only it wasn't sweet; it was like biting an inner tube soaked in turpentine. We also mauled chunks of paraffin left over from sealing jelly jars. Later, in the city, we discovered the delights of road tar, foul, dirty and darkly satisfying. We could even black out our incisors with it and pretend the bully on the block had removed our front teeth, which brought anguished shrieks from our mothers and I'm-glad-smarty grins from our sisters.

Modern gum was born in the United States about 1869, thanks to General Santa Anna. He had contacted American inventor Thomas Adams hoping the man could turn chicle into a substitute for rubber. The general arrived chewing the stuff, and Adams immediately saw it was superior to any then-known chewing-gum base. In a few years, Adams' Chiclets began appearing on the scene.

Chicle is basically latex. Some latexes—*latex* being a generic term—are *sorva* and *leche caspi* from the Amazon Valley; *tunu* and *nispero* from Central America, and *jelutong*, found in Malaya and Indonesia. But juice from the 100-foot-tall sapodilla tree of the Yucatan peninsula is still the main source of chicle. Tapped only after they're a quarter-century old, a cutting yields about two-and-a-half pounds of gum base, and it's three years before they can be "bled" again.

Some Sweet Marvels

As a kid, my loyalty was about equally divided between bubble gum and penny candy. Gum was great, but popularity was assured anyone whose pockets held candy, too. In those days we had such marvels as Queen Anne Butterballs, Walnettos, jawbreakers, tootsie rolls (no kid worth his salt ever capitalized tootsie rolls; heck, they were family), and little banana-flavored squares in yellow wax paper whose name I forget. No, wait, I've got it—*KITS!* Kits gave you four or five or seven individual hunks for a PENNY. Such bounty could only have bankrupted whomever made them, which must be why they aren't around any more.

And, oh yes, you could also get real baby Baby Ruths and Snickers and Three Musketeers bars for a penny.

I never could get enough candy. I swore to best friends, who joined me in my oath, that when I grew up I'd have all the candy that I ever wanted. But life is full of surprises. How could I know then that I'd change, as we all do?

As little boys, we love candy. As grown men in a world that sometimes seems unhappy, sometimes insecure and unfamiliar, surely it isn't odd that we wonder if we can still have even a little of that Willy Wonka world.

And if we find it, is it worth more than a penny?

Watching the Watchdog

Sara Bren

Out our way in a vacant lot
    There's a tree that has a *SECRET* spot.
I'm not supposed to leave the yard,
    But Gruff, the pup, is standing guard.

    When it's too hot to run and play,
        I spend the best part of the day
    High in the treetop, looking down,
        Before my naptime comes around.

Sometimes I act like I'm a spy
    And wear a black patch on my eye;
Or hold my magic viewing glass
    To watch the people as they pass.

I see the town come into view,
    With power lines and towers, too.
The Freeway Flyer has to rush
    To meet the big, green, city bus.

    A traffic 'copter hurries by
        Just like a giant dragonfly.
    Then I pretend I'm lost at sea
        And hope the pilot rescues me.

The world seems busy all around—
    Planes in the air, trains on the ground.
I wish my magic glass would show
    Where all the trucks and trailers go.

Someday when I have grown a lot,
    I may outgrow this *SECRET* spot.
Right now, I'd best go down and see
    If Gruff the watchdog's watching me.

Brotherhood is hand stretching out to hand,
It's unity—a never-ending stretch of land,
It's souls caring,
It's people sharing,
It's minds understanding minds,
Realizing it takes all kinds.

Julia Dawn Locke

Brotherhood

Of all the gifts the gods bestow
The greatest gift we humans know,
The sweetest joy, the highest good
Of life itself is brotherhood.

Brotherhood is burden-bearing,
Loving, lifting, helping, sharing
Every load a brother bears,
Every pain his sad heart wears.

Brotherhood is comradeship
Of the heart and life and lip,
Comradeship by day and night,
Brown and yellow, black and white.

From whence hath come this wonder thing,
This rich reward for clown and king?
How shall we know the password, pray,
When Comrade Christ shall come our way?

Thus shall we know, O friend of mine;
Thus shall we greet the Great Divine;
Thus shall we feel this faith so true;
This comradeship long overdue:

Brotherhood is reaching out
With a handclasp and a shout
Of friendliness, a God-like birth
Of helpfulness around the earth!

William L. Stidger

Garden in the Sun

Grace Noll Crowell

Here is a woman's labor come to birth,
Here she is repaid for time and toil;
A blinding brilliance overflows the earth
And runs like light above the broken soil.

The heady phlox, the flaming marigolds,
The pungent gay nasturtiums in their bed
Toss in the wind—one single poppy holds
Color enough to dye the landscape red.

A woman's hands, a garden—a few seed,
And a wealth at last to meet the spirit's need.

Dawn in the Garden

Sometimes I rose at dawn and stole into the garden while the heavy dew lay on the grass and flowers. Few know what joy it is to feel the roses pressing softly into the hand, or the beautiful motion of the lilies as they sway in the morning breeze. Sometimes I caught an insect in the flower I was plucking, and I felt the faint noise of a pair of wings rubbed together in a sudden terror, as the little creature became aware of a pressure from without.

Another favorite haunt of mine was the orchard, where the fruit ripened in early July. The large, downy peaches would reach themselves into my hands, and as the joyous breezes flew about the trees the apples tumbled at my feet. Oh, the delight with which I gathered up the fruit in my pinafore, pressed my face against the smooth cheeks of the apples, still warm from the sun, and skipped back to the house!

Helen Keller

Thanks for Sharing

"Hello, everybody. This is Kate Smith," was the famous line that greeted America and introduced one of the leading radio personalities of the 1930s and 1940s. The patriotism, down-home philosophy and glorious voice of Kate Smith were an inspiration to millions. This was especially true during the war years when she sold more war bonds through marathons than any other American entertainer.

Kathryn (Kate) Elizabeth Smith was born May 1, 1909 in Greenville, Virginia to William and Charlotte Smith. They later moved to Washington D.C., where Kate grew up with her sister, Helene. Kate, blessed with perfect pitch and rhythm, loved to sing, starting at the age of four with her church choir. When she was eight years old, General John J. Pershing gave her a medal for morale-boosting for singing to the troops during World War I.

Her parents felt she should go into nursing. Kate was miserable studying to be a nurse; her heart just wasn't in it. She entered amateur shows on weekends and won, until she was hired for a week by the manager of the theater. The producer of the Broadway show "Honeymoon Lane" heard her sing and offered her a contract for the part of Tiny Little. The show ran for two years, then she went on to do "Hit the Deck" and then "Flying High." Although Kate loved singing and the audience, her parts in these shows brought her more misery than pleasure, for she had been cast for her size, not her voice, and she bore the brunt of the jokes. Almost at the end of the run of "Flying High," when Kate was most disheartened, her father died. The loss of her father and the cruel jokes about her weight were almost too much to bear. Kate seriously thought about leaving the stage forever. She still loved to sing, but didn't want to be in another musical. That's when Ted Collins heard her performance in "Flying High" and had her cut a record for Columbia Phonographic Company, of which he was an executive. He talked to Kate about managing her career; they shook hands and from that point she sang and he managed. After the play "Flying High" closed, Ted got Kate an audition for the president of Columbia Broadcasting System, and she was given a fifteen minute spot—opposite "Amos 'n Andy." By the late 1930s she and Jack Benny had the only noncancelable contracts in radio.

Ted left Columbia and he and Kate formed the Kated Corporation which produced the Kate Smith weekly hour program, six "Kate Smith Speaks" daily talk shows and several other radio acts, such as the "Aldrich Family" and "My Son and I." Her theme song was "When the Moon Comes Over the Mountain."

In 1938 Irving Berlin gave her exclusive rights to sing "God Bless America" which became so popular, a movement got under way to have the song replace the "Star Spangled Banner" as the national anthem. Kate was also asked by President Franklin D. Roosevelt to give a command performance for visiting King George VI and Queen Elizabeth of England, at which the President introduced her as "This is Kate Smith—this is America."

During her radio career, Kate's audience was primarily women. In her talk shows, she brought a homespun philosophy about events and matters of interest to women, their families, and their homes. Her positive attitudes and genuine interest in people endeared her to many. Her audiences felt as if she were a part of their families, someone who cared.

In 1950 Kate made her television debut with "The Kate Smith Hour." Six years later Ted suffered a heart attack, and they cancelled all further commitments. It wasn't until 1959 that Kate returned to television with a variety program and Ted as executive producer. Kate went on to do a concert debut in Carnegie Hall and to appear in nightclubs. She cut well over two thousand recordings, nineteen sold over one million each.

After their long and close relationship, in which Ted made all the decisions concerning her career, his death in 1964 came as a terrible blow. Thereafter, Kate has only appeared as a guest on variety shows and specials.

Kate Smith touched millions with her honesty and caring. Expressing the appreciation she felt for her audiences, she closed her shows with "Thanks for listening." America says, "Thanks for sharing." Shari Style

OUR COUNTRY

Anna Louise Dabney

Our country is a tapestry,
Woven by loving hands;
By Faith and Hope 'twas deftly made
From threads of other lands;

And each retains its native hue
Whose beauty animates
A varied pattern, lovely, new—
Our own United States.

THE MELTING POT

Thomas Curtis Clark

When brave Ulysses left his native isle
    To sail the shining main, to seek new shores
And unknown countries, bursting golden doors
    To fair new realms that basked in Summer's smile,
He saw no stranger sights than we today
    In these our city streets, where earth has poured
From every farthest land her human horde:

    Proud Nipponese, sojourners from Cathay,
    Shrewd Greeks, and Turks, and roving Syrians;
    Gay Spanish dons and dour Scotch peasantry,
    High-hearted French, dark rogues from Barbary;
    No race or breed is barred by selfish bans.
    Here, where the dream of liberty had birth,
    God dreams His dream, democracy for earth.

"The Melting-Pot" from HOME ROADS AND FAR HORIZONS
by Thomas Curtis Clark. Copyright 1935 by Harper & Row,
Publishers, Inc. Reprinted by permission of the publisher.

COLOR ART AND PHOTO CREDITS
(in order of appearance)

Front and back covers, Grand Teton Range and Snake River, Wyoming, Colour Library International (USA) Limited; inside front and back covers, Palouse Farming Country, Washington, Colour Library International (USA) Limited; Desert sunrise, Josef Muench; Mountain lake, H. Armstrong Roberts; Begonia, Freelance Photographers Guild; Carmel Mission, California, Josef Muench; Minuteman statue, Freelance Photographers Guild; Patriotic painting, Three Lions, Inc.; Sailboat near Stonington, Maine, Bob Taylor; Vermont countryside, Bob Taylor; Back Cove, New Harbor, Maine, Fred Sieb; Clinton Mill, New Jersey, Gene Ahrens; Ingalls dining room, Laura Ingalls Wilder Memorial Society, Inc., DeSmet, South Dakota; THE PRAIRIE IS MY GARDEN, Harvey Dunn, South Dakota Memorial Art Center Collection, Brookings; Lupines, H. Armstrong Roberts; Bridge at Warner, New Hampshire, Fred Sieb; TOM SAWYER AND HUCKLEBERRY FINN, Gannam, Three Lions, Inc.; Ecola State Park near Cannon Beach, Oregon, Ed Cooper; Church near Middle Ridge, Wisconsin, Ken Dequaine; Sagamore Hill, National Park Service, photo by Richard Frear; Statue of Liberty, New York City, H. Armstrong Roberts; In the garden, H. Armstrong Roberts; Whitecombe Garden, Cotuit, Cape Cod, Massachusetts, Freelance Photographers Guild; Formal garden, Gerald Koser; Windmill at Solvang, Santa Ynez Valley, California, Josef Muench.

ACKNOWLEDGMENTS

OUR COUNTRY by Anna Louise Dabney. From MY AMERICAN HERITAGE published by Rand McNally & Company. NEW ENGLAND TOWN and VILLAGE BY THE SEA by Ruth Linnea Erickson. From HOMESPUN VERSE by Ruth Linnea Erickson. Copyright © 1956 by Ruth Linnea Erickson. BEAUTY by Hazelle R. Paus. From JOURNEYS IN THOUGHTLAND by Hazelle R. Paus. Copyright 1955 by Hazelle R. Paus. A LESSON IN JULY by John Fred Schilling. From STRONG COUNTRY by John Fred Schilling. Copyright © 1967 by John Fred Schilling. Published by Dorrance & Company. THE AMERICAN FLAG and THEY WALKED HERE by Helen Shick. From POEMS FROM THIS VALLEY by Helen Shick. BROTHERHOOD by William L. Stidger. From I SAW GOD WASH THE WORLD, Copyright © 1934 by William L. Stidger. Used with permission of William S. Hyland. Excerpt from THE ADVENTURES OF TOM SAWYER by Mark Twain (Childrens Press Edition). Used by permission of Childrens Press.

Autumn's finest gift . . .

Autumn Ideals portrays the vibrant fall season in brilliant color photography and keepsake art reproductions. An outstanding selection of poetry highlights the attributes of favorite fall flowers, the bounties of the harvest and the changing colors of the rural countryside.

Enjoy a touching article entitled "The Letter," written by a father to his daughter as she leaves for college. Savor the natural sweetness of a variety of fruits in delicious recipes featured in "Fruits of Autumn." Celebrate the richness of the season with the people of America as they welcome autumn throughout our land.

Enrich the lives of loved ones and special friends with a gift subscription to Ideals! Subscribe for yourself and treasure the pictorial splendor of Ideals all year long!